FRITZI FOX

FLEW IN FROM FLORIDA

FROM FLORIDA

by Leah Komaiko

illustrations by Thacher Hurd

A Laura Geringer Book

An Imprint of HarperCollins*Publishers*

To Bird and Tim, and Fritzi—
wherever you are
—L.K.

For Marilyn Marlow
—T.H.

Fritzi Fox Flew In From Florida
Text copyright © 1995 by Leah Komaiko
Illustrations copyright © 1995 by Thacher Hurd
Printed in Mexico. All rights reserved.

Library of Congress Cataloging-in-Publication Data
Komaiko, Leah.
    Fritzi Fox flew in from Florida / by Leah Komaiko ; illustrated by Thacher Hurd.
        p.   cm.
    "A Laura Geringer book."
    Summary: Shy and quiet when she first arrives from Florida for an overnight visit,
Fritzi Fox soon reveals some very exciting aspects to her personality as she transforms
her host's bedroom into a tropical paradise.
    ISBN 0-06-021506-2. — ISBN 0-06-021507-0 (lib. bdg.)
    [1. Stories in rhyme.]   1. Hurd, Thacher, ill.   II. Title.
PZ8.3.K835Fr   1995   93-4754
[E]—dc20   CIP
                                                                            AC

Typography by Al Cetta
1 2 3 4 5 6 7 8 9 10
❖
First Edition

Is Florida very far away?

Fritzi Fox flew in from Florida—
That's her walking off the flight.

She's just like us—with a tan face
And a fourteen-ton straw suitcase. . . .
Fritzi's come to spend one night.

Fritzi Fox flew in from Florida—
She's never been here before.
On her hat—an orange is growing!
On our street it won't stop snowing.
Now she's walking in our door.

I have never flown to Florida—
Mom says nothing's there but sun.
Something tells me—
Follow Fritzi. . . .

But Fritzi Fox is very quiet.
Won't dance—says it starts a riot.
Can't sing—she's too shy to try it.
Just eats eggs, she's on a diet.

Then she yawns and pats her mouth —
"It seems," she says,
"I'm slipping south.
I'm much too sleepy to unpack —
Excuse me while I hit the sack."

Now I know Florida's boring:
Next thing I'll hear Fritzi snoring.

Fritzi has a house in Florida,
Where she sleeps facing the sea.
But tonight, I said it's all right
If she shares my room with me.

Then Dad shuts off the light.
He says, "Sweet dreams"
    and "Sleep tight."
It's me and her in here all night.

Wait!
Fritzi's up and at her suitcase.
Can't sleep, she says, in a dark place.

Hey!
You could use a little sand dune.

How about a blue lagoon?
Monkeys, palm trees,
A beach needs a sea breeze.

Bring in the birds and butterflies—
Big ones, twice your size.

In your bed you'll find one alligator —
Oh, are there more?
Did I bring four?

Seashells, surf swells,
We all need some seaweed.

And once a day I eat this dish —
Peanuts and jellyfish.

I love to do the mambo,

Sing songs with my combo.

Even when we sleep I have the notion
Nothing *ever* sleeps under the ocean.

Fritzi Fox flew in from Florida—
She's flying back home today.
Something tells me,
Someday I'll see Florida—
It's not far away.